THE BRITISH RENAISSANCE 1979–?

The Francis Boyer Lectures on Public Policy

THE BRITISH RENAISSANCE 1979 –?

Alan Walters

American Enterprise Institute for Public Policy Research

ISBN 0-8447-1367-8

Library of Congress Catalog Card No. 83-073453

Printed in the United States of America

American Enterprise Institute
1150 Seventeenth Street, N.W., Washington, D.C. 20036

THE
FRANCIS BOYER LECTURES
ON PUBLIC POLICY

The American Enterprise Institute has initiated the Francis Boyer Lectures on Public Policy to examine the relationship between business and government and to develop contexts for their creative interaction. These lectures have been made possible by an endowment from the SmithKline Beckman Corporation in memory of Mr. Boyer, the late chairman of the board of the corporation.

The lecture is given by an eminent thinker who has developed notable insights on one or more aspects of the relationship between the nation's private and public sectors. Focusing clearly on the public interest, the lecture demonstrates how new conceptual insights may illuminate public policy issues and contribute significantly to the dialogue by which the public interest is served.

The man or woman delivering the lecture need not necessarily be a professional scholar, a government official, or a business leader. The lecture would concern itself with the central issues of public policy in contemporary America—pointing always in the direction of constructive solutions rather than merely delineating opposing views.

Lecturers may come from any walk of life—academia, the humanities, public service, science, finance, the mass media of communications, business, and industry.

The principal considerations determining the selection are the quality and appositeness of the lecturer's thought, rather than his or her formal qualifications.

The Francis Boyer Lecture is delivered annually in Washington, D.C., before an invited audience. The lecturer is selected by the American Enterprise Institute's distinguished Council of Academic Advisers, and the lectureship carries an award and stipend of $10,000. The American Enterprise Institute publishes the lecture as the Francis Boyer Lectures on Public Policy.

Francis Boyer Award Recipients

1977   *The Honorable Gerald R. Ford*
1978   *The Honorable Arthur F. Burns*
1979   *Paul Johnson*
1980   *William J. Baroody, Sr.*
1981   *The Honorable Henry A. Kissinger*
1982   *Hanna Holborn Gray*
1983   *Sir Alan Walters*

FOREWORD

Sir Alan Arthur Walters, former economic adviser to British Prime Minister Margaret Thatcher, has been named by the American Enterprise Institute's Council of Academic Advisers as the seventh recipient of the Francis Boyer Award, given annually to an eminent thinker who has gained notable insights into public policy. The award is named for the late chairman of the SmithKline Beckman Corporation.

Sir Alan joins a distinguished group of recipients: former President Gerald R. Ford, Ambassador Arthur F. Burns, British historian Paul Johnson, the late William J. Baroody, Sr., former Secretary of State Henry Kissinger, and University of Chicago President Hanna Holborn Gray.

In 1979, Prime Minister Thatcher was elected on a platform that promised to alter radically the course of the British economy. After twenty years of rising inflation, growing nationalization, and expanding regulation, the new Conservative government took office determined to reverse those trends.

Sir Alan, who joined AEI as a resident scholar in international economics when he left the Thatcher government, explains in this Francis Boyer Lecture the past failures of British economic policy and assesses the reforms introduced by Mrs. Thatcher to rejuvenate the British economy. He identifies some of the factors that are perceived to be root causes of the loss of vitality in the pre-Thatcher

British economy. Among these are excessive wage demands by trade unions and the growing concentration of market power by a few firms in key industries. Pre-Thatcher governments, with their accommodating demand policies and lack of credibility, also played a major role in the economic decline.

Thatcher policies, Sir Alan says, sought to establish credibility. Instead of the government giving in to excessive demands by trade unions, he says, the private sector now has to accommodate the firm policy of the government. Financial control was set in place, and budget deficits as a percentage of the gross national product were reduced. Rates of taxation have diminished progressively so as to restore incentives. Regulatory controls on industry and social welfare were reduced, and a move has been made to sell off nationalized industries to private ownership. Assessing the costs and benefits of the Thatcher program, Sir Alan contends that these policies have set the course for a renaissance of the British economy.

Sir Alan is a professor of economics at Johns Hopkins University, a position he held before becoming the prime minister's economic adviser. He was an economic adviser to the World Bank, Cassel Professor of Economics at the London School of Economics, and professor and head of the department of econometrics at the University of Birmingham.

He also served as visiting professor of economics at Northwestern University, the University of Oregon, the University of Virginia, and Monash University, and was Visiting Ford Professor at the Massachusetts Institute of Technology. He is a fellow of the International Economic Society and of Nuffield College, Oxford.

Sir Alan was joint managing editor of the *Review of Economic Studies,* a member of the editorial board of the

Journal of Urban Economics, and the author of numerous books and articles on economics and microeconomics, including *Microeconomic Theory, Money and Banking, Money in Boom and Slump,* and *Growth without Development.*

The American Enterprise Institute is honored to have this highly respected scholar in residence and to present him with the Francis Boyer Award. We are also grateful to the SmithKline Beckman Corporation for making possible the Francis Boyer Award and Lecture, one of many ways in which AEI fosters the competition of ideas so vital to a free society.

Bill Baroody Jr.

WILLIAM J. BAROODY, JR.

President
American Enterprise Institute

xi

THE BRITISH RENAISSANCE 1979-?

POLITICAL PRELUDE

Only a few months ago, the free Western world breathed a long sigh of relief. Mrs. Thatcher's Conservative government had been decisively reelected. One of the linchpins of the Western alliance was once again firmly in place. The fear of a Labour victory—which promised unilateralism in defense, a potty kind of pacificism in foreign policy, and inflationary finance with bureaucratic controls on the economy—was finally dispelled, for at least four years.

The subtleties and stupidities of the election campaign are, to a large extent, far beyond my comprehension. And I can readily resist the temptation to pontificate on the polls. But one conclusion is inescapable: the British public decisively rejected rampant socialism.

Although by the early months of 1983 it was clear that a Conservative victory, even a landslide, was on the cards, it had not always been so. Certainly in the winter of 1980–1981, when I returned to London, a Conservative defeat looked all but certain. The betting during the first half of 1981 was all on the New Alliance of the old Liberal and nascent Social Democratic party. Never was a marriage celebrated with such fond hopes and such great expectations.

The Alliance was the natural heir to all that was good and to that dominant consensus—between the paternalistic wings of the Conservative party and the traditional center-right of the Labour party (Butskelism in its economic policies, reflecting the two chancellors, R. A. Butler and Hugh Gaitskell, Conservative and Labour respectively, who laid the foundation of the consensus in the 1950s)—that had ruled Britain for more than thirty years. Yet in June the electors rejected the cosy consensus of the Alliance even more firmly than the socialism of Labour.

The reelection of Mrs. Thatcher confirms what many had hitherto only suspected: there has been a decisive change in the structure of British politics. If the government of Mrs. Thatcher had lost or if there had been a hung Parliament, then the Conservative leadership would undoubtedly have changed. The wets would have won. Losers lose all in politics. The 1979–1983 Thatcher government would have been adduced as convincing evidence that fundamental reform of the British economy would always founder on the obstinacy and ignorance of the electorate. Only a reckless politician would use up good political capital on hopeless ventures of reform. Thus the Tory party would have been wrapped again in its paternalist trappings. The slow road to serfdom would be the only way.

Well, the ninth of June changed all that. For a while—and I believe for a long while—the British are now finally on the road toward a free society shaped by individual liberty and moral responsibility.

THE RECORD AND THE REFORMS

The cornerstone of Mrs. Thatcher's policies from 1979 onward was economic reform. There was wide agreement among all people and parties that *some* reform was needed. Calculations of growth, productivity, trade, and income showed that, although Britain had been a leader of Europe in interwar years, the decades after World War II had seen poor Britain struggling at the bottom of the league. While Britain had been disposing of an empire, she had also lost much of her economic vitality. To Britons who had long regarded "Europeans" as poverty-stricken peasants, the greater affluence of the continent was galling. Foreign goods supplanted British in places that had long been the preserve of British industry. By the end of the 1950s Britain had replaced France as the "sick man of Europe."

Diagnoses of the British disease by learned doctors as well as quacks ranged from the quixotic to the queer. But there were some common denominators of concern. First there was wide agreement that the peculiar British trades unions were one important underlying cause of the backwardness of Britain. Archaic work practices, reminiscent of the rituals of strange religions long lost in the mists of antiquity, were jealously preserved. The state abided and abetted by rendering the funds of trades unions immune; the unions (along with the queen) cannot be sued for breach of contract. This substantial privilege has not been left unexploited.

At various times in the postwar years, attempts have been made by both Labour and Conservative governments to outlaw the more outrageous abuses of union power and even to make the unions accountable for their actions. All failed. The union barons flexed their muscles and were duly appeased. In the latter half of the 1970s it really did appear that Britain was ruled by these barons—and it was widely predicted that they would be just as much the undoing of Mrs. Thatcher as they were the blight of British business. At the very least, it was thought, they would impose wage demands that would be the ruin of any Conservative economic strategy.

A second cause of British decline was thought to be that the market for British goods was too restricted and British firms were too small to enjoy the great technological economies of scale that were just there for the merging. The size-of-market argument thus provided a rationalization for entering the EEC. And the size-of-firm complaint gave rise to governments officiating at shotgun mergers and other more or less incestuous arrangements.

To any objective observer, all this posturing about markets and size may seem rather odd. The size of the domestic market (or indeed the size of firm), for example, does not appear markedly to have inhibited the prosperity of industry in Switzerland, Sweden, Austria, or, say, Lichtenstein. Furthermore, the statistics showed that Britain already seemed to have the *largest* size of firm, measured by employment, in the OECD countries. Industrial elephantiasis was more likely the problem than the cure.

But it would be quite wrong to think that such reflections on reason and evidence would in any way affect the decisions of policy makers. Socialists, with their union paymasters, profess to hate big business but are really closet lovers of those large firms. The bigger the firm, the easier to organize labor, on the one hand, and for government to control, on the other. Similarly Tory paternalists found it much more agreeable to twist the arms of the chairmen of a few megasloths than to chase thousands of rugged little entrepreneurs who would be likely to turn a deaf ear if not a profane tongue.[1] With industry duly concentrated, there was at least some chance of imposing price and wage controls or what was to be called "industrial" or "indicative" planning.

The Socialist governments (and less enthusiastically

the Conservative governments) have always contended that the salvation of Britain lay in more planning. They observed the unexpected renaissance of France from 1958 onward and attributed this *rassemblement* to the planning of industrial development by the Commissariat du Plan. Alas, not for the first time, Britain had confused French rhetoric with reality. As with all planning systems, there is a deep, wide, foggy gulf between the professions of planners and plans and the performance of plants and people. But willy-nilly the success of de Gaulle's new republic gave a great impetus to planning in Britain during the late 1950s and early 1960s.[2]

One essential ingredient was the apparent way in which the French planned aggregate demand and industrial output. While the British *squeezed* the French seemed to *smooth* demand. It seemed that entrepreneurs in France had more or less ensured expanding markets. What Britain needed was to keep aggregate demand ever expanding. Instead of a "stop-go" economy, what everyone wanted in the swinging sixties was a "go-go" Britain. We could, so to speak, grow out of our constraints. Growth solves all always.

And so it would. But the very growth so dear to all governments proved to be elusive. Even worse, the more determined the attempts to expand demand, the more miserable the performance. For fifteen years, from Reginald Maudling's ebullient "go-for-growth" policy of 1963 through to the final cramps of Mr. Callaghan's "winter of discontent" in 1978–1979, governments, following prestigious economic advice, had periodically administered large doses of demand to induce growth. After some transitory signs of expansion, which became shorter and shorter as the fifteen years elapsed, the economy always settled back into an even more slothful state than before. The combination of massive budget deficits and monetary accommodation produced not only near-stagnation (about 1 percent per annum growth) but also a record rate of inflation of about 15 percent during the 1970s.[3] Nor did the go-go policy solve the perennial problem of rising unemployment. The percentage of unemployed seemed to double roughly every seven years.

Just like the go-go girls, the go-go men had (to a deafening chorus of approval from the economics profession) postured long and promised much; they delivered, however, only a faint dying flicker of excitement followed by disappointed expectations and much resentment in a disgruntled electorate.[4]

The 1979 Conservative program was the antithesis of the disintegrating consensus. The predominant characteristic of governments before Mrs. Thatcher was their accommodating flexibility. Pre-Thatcher governments, both Labour and Conservative, were not encumbered with ideological baggage. They were pragmatists. They eschewed ideologies. They shifted their policies, and the grounds on which they justified them, with quite remarkable adeptness. After all, it was argued, circumstances change: and so policies should be adapted *flexibly* to take on board the new conditions.[5]

One of the perennial problems of the British economy, for example, was the overweening wage demands—particularly by the all-powerful union barons in the great nationalized industries. After a ritual huff and puff, governments normally caved in to the demands. The enlarged wage bill was "accommodated," for such is the euphemism, by increased budget deficits and ultimately by an increased money supply.[6]

In short, governments yielded. Such "flexibility" of government, however, did not stimulate flexibility among trades unions, firms, and pressure groups. On the contrary, the more flexible the government, the more rigid the demands of the private sector. If the government would endlessly accommodate the status quo and the outrageous wage demands of powerful unions, then there was little incentive to change and no real restraint on wage demands.

Mrs. Thatcher's policy was to replace this wobbly jellolike flexibility with firmness and resolution. Then instead of government's adapting to the inconsistent demands of the captains of industry and barons of the unions, the private sector would have to accommodate to the firm policy of government.

Hitherto flexibility in government had bred rigidity in the private sector; henceforth rigidity in government would foster flexibility in the private sector.

But the private sector of industry was only part of the problem—and certainly the easiest to solve. The dominant cause of the rigidity of the economy was the public sector industries—steel, coal, railways, electricity, gas, shipbuilding. These great industries were nationalized by Labour governments intent, as they said, on "securing the commanding heights of the economy." Socialist theorists thought that with such commanding heights under control the government would be able to regulate most of the economy. Alas, it turned out just the opposite. Instead of commanding the nationalized industries, governments were largely commanded by them. The graffiti expressed it succinctly: "Miners Rule, O.K.?"[7]

THE POLICY AND THE PERFORMANCE

In essence the Thatcher policy was set out in a series of rules or, as her political enemies would call them, doctrinaire rigidities.

First, and fundamental, was financial control. In Britain this implied not only control over the money supply but also a persistent downward trend in the budget deficits (as a fraction of GNP). *Second*, state spending was to be reduced to an extent that allowed rates of taxation to be progressively diminished so as to restore incentives and enterprise. *Third*, there was to be a reduction in controls and regulations in both firms and families. *Fourth*, there was to be a progressive policy of selling off the nationalized industries and returning them to private ownership and control.

So what is the score so far?[8]

On the first objective, financial control, I would judge the performance to be very good—scoring perhaps eight or even nine points out of a possible ten. Britain is one of the few countries—perhaps the only country!—in OECD that does not have a budget deficit problem. It is under control and on track. Furthermore, during the last target period, 1982–1983, all the target monetary aggregates were within the specified range.

Over the first two years, of course, monetary and fiscal policy never did have so smooth a ride. Yet with all the oscillations, which were incidentally not nearly as violent as those experienced here, the slow (5 percent) growth of the monetary base over the four years ensured that inflation would fall from its peak of 23 percent in mid-1980 to the 5 percent experienced today. The proof of the pudding indeed.[9]

On the second objective, the reduction of spending and taxes, the score of the first four years is much lower—a modest five out of ten is appropriate. The British government found it difficult to arrest the growth of public spending. Of course, from 1979 to 1981 much of the increase in public spending was due to the transition from the top of the boom in 1979 to the depths of the depression in 1981. In fact, comparing the *slump* years of 1974–1975 and 1975–1976, public spending as a percentage of GDP actually *fell* from 46 percent to 44.5 percent in 1981–1982. Not much, perhaps, and certainly not enough, but nevertheless a fall.[10]

A perhaps charitable view of this performance is rather like the judgment passed by Dr. Johnson, who was not notorious for his charity, comparing a "woman's preaching" to the dog that walked on its back legs: "It is not done well; but you are surprised to find it done at all." Under the pressures of the slump, it was surprising that *anything* was achieved in restraining spending.

The underlying and continuing cause of the relentless rise of public spending is the "demand-driven" expenditures or, as they are called in the United States, the "entitlement programs." Over the century during which the welfare state had been steadily expanding, one service after another, which used to be considered the responsibility of the family or individual, has been absorbed as a matter for the state. The individual has been treated more like a child. He cannot be relied upon to provide for education, ill-health, and retirement; the state must act as a nanny and do it for him. Thus the state relieves the individual of a substantial fraction of his income to operate the state welfare services, leaving him with mere pocket money, which is, so to speak, all he can be trusted with.

The government of 1979–1983 put a brake on the creation of new entitlements and new programs.[11] It did something, but not very much, to arrest the rapid natural growth of existing welfare and other services. But just as in the United States and many other Western democracies, this remains the most serious unfinished business. Unless the burden be relieved, the West will be the first civilization to collapse under the weight of its good intentions.

The only way to avoid this Armageddon is to persuade the public of the damnable arithmetic of these programs. Voters must be convinced that such burdens will fall on those whom they cherish—their children.

Meanwhile, the burgeoning public programs have to be paid for out of taxation or borrowing. In the first Thatcher government the burden of taxation increased, particularly in the tough 1981 budget. In a great act of statesmanship, the chancellor and the prime minister decided that since they could not reduce public spending, they must nevertheless finance it "honestly" through increases in taxes. They eschewed both inflationary finance, by "printing" money, and increased borrowing, with consequential tax increases in future years. The reward came later. In both 1982 and 1983 the chancellor was able to reduce taxes substantially yet maintain the principle of "honest finance." Taxes are still expected to be reduced rather than increased.

Yet anticipations of really impressive reductions in tax rates in the second Thatcher government are much constrained by the likely path of public spending . . . and so we are back once more at the central problem of the next decade—those entitlements.

On the third objective, the reduction of regulation, I would score a relatively high seven out of ten. The program began most auspiciously—"at a stroke" Mrs. Thatcher abolished exchange controls in 1979. The elimination of wages and price controls (except for certain minimum wage legislation controlled by unbreakable international treaty and, most important, for rent control on private sector dwellings) also followed quickly upon the election. Deregulation worked; and it was obvious it worked well. There was no popular demand for the reinstatement of these controls.

With the last objective, the program of denationalization, we can score not more than six out of ten. The main criticism is that it has proceeded too slowly. There is a basic difficulty. The Labour party threatened that if elected a Labour government would renationalize without compensation. Such uncertainties, combined with the slump, have

obviously much inhibited sales of publicly owned corporations.[12] Yet in the second Thatcher government the signs
are auspicious. Many of the great nationalized concerns will
be sold off and subject to the private disciplines of the
market. Some hope that this policy will undo the great
damage inflicted on British industry since the first great
wave of nationalization from 1945 to 1950.

For the individual, the most obvious and successful
measure is the continuing sale, at a discount, of publicly
owned housing to the sitting tenants. This is a most imme-
diate and potent way of returning property to the people.
Furthermore, no future Labour government will *dare* to dis-
possess these new owners.[13] So far some 600,000 houses
have been sold—but this is slightly less than 10 percent of
the total of public housing. There is still a long way to go.

Unemployment as the Cost?

Now you may judge this as a record of solid if spotty achieve-
ment. But what about the costs of Thatcherism? The most
obvious—and what would seem to be politically the most
damaging—is the increase in unemployment from about 1.3
million in 1979 to more than 3 million in 1983: from 5.5
percent to more than 13 percent. *Industrial* production had
also declined precipitously—by the spring of 1981 it had
fallen 14 percent since the election in May 1979. True,
industrial production started rising from mid-1981 onward,
and the service industries expanded fairly steadily throughout the four years, but many of the great traditional industrial areas remain depressed, with an increasing number of
long-term unemployed.

Mrs. Thatcher suffered from a singular handicap;
she came into office in 1979 at the top of the boom. The
only way to go was down. It is therefore a little misleading to

use the boom year as the basis for the discussion of achievements (or the lack of them!).[14] We should always compare trough with trough or peak with peak. Comparing industrial production at the bottom of the cycle in 1981 with the last cycle's trough figure in 1975, we find that, in spite of the more severe world slump, output never sank below the level of the previous slump. *Indeed total gross domestic product was about 6.5 percent more in 1981 than it was in the slump of 1975.*[15]

But Mrs. Thatcher's policies were not concerned merely with the temporary cyclical surges in output. The measures were aimed at long-term reforms. Signs that the old order was changing, giving place to new, appeared from 1981 onward. The statistics began to show that there was a remarkable, unexpected, and countercyclical increase in productivity.[16] These statistics are corroborated by the reports from the sharp end of industry. Managers are said to be at last managing, instead of delegating decisions to shop stewards (local union organizers). Anecdotes of wonders abound; for example, productivity in the steel and chemical industries in 1983 was reported to exceed that in Germany. Anyone who has spoken with British businessmen over the last two or three years will soon be convinced that there has been a fundamental change in attitude, application, and determination. Of course, no one can foresee how long this change will persist. As soon as the economy expands rapidly, it is said, old habits will reassert themselves, and Britain will be back in the dumps once more. Perhaps so—but I suspect that such Jeremiahs will be just as confounded then as they have been over the years since 1981.

But granted that the output picture is, if not actually glowing brightly, then not nearly so dark as it is painted, one cannot deny that the unemployment scene is distinctly more gloomy. This is so. But to assert that it is mainly due to

Mrs. Thatcher's policies requires more than an avowal of the faith.[17]

My argument is the opposite of the conventional one. I think that unemployment is so large not because of Thatcherism from 1979 on but primarily because the Thatcherite policies started *too late* (that is, from 1981 onward) *and took some time to carry conviction and establish credibility.* Most governments waste the first year or so, and the 1979–1983 government was no exception (as Sir Keith Joseph remarked at the time). In my judgment the government did not get a firm grip on budgetary policy until the spring of 1981. Yet the greatest *absolute* increase in the numbers unemployed occurred in 1980—during a year when the budget deficit, as a percentage of GDP, *rose* (from 5.1 to 5.7). In 1981 and 1982 (and I forecast for 1983) the absolute increase in unemployment declined.[18]

It is illogical to blame the policies of 1981 for the events of 1980.[19] The proximate explanation of the rapid increase of unemployment in 1980 continuing into 1981 was the virtual doubling of the percentage increase in wages and salaries from 1977 to 1979 and continuing throughout 1980 at over 20 percent. Clearly few people believed that the inflation would be tamed. Almost everyone—and that included solid labor negotiators as well as the garrulous journalists—expected a reflationary budget in 1981, whatever the professions of the chancellor and the prime minister may have been. The cynical view was: "Of course, they are bound to say they are sticking to their policies while they are in process of changing them." Thus, on this view, the large increases in money wages would again have been inflated away, and Britain would have been back once more on its familiar spiral of prices chasing costs.

In short, until 1981 the policy of the government lacked the most essential ingredient—credibility. After

1981 the message had penetrated even the thickest skulls. The government meant what it said.

In 1977-1979 wage bargains (at over 20 percent) had already been struck on the expectation that the inflation would balloon again. In 1981-1982, however, it became clear that inflation was falling rapidly. So labor, with almost stable prices of output yet rapidly increasing wage rates, priced itself out of much of the competitive market. At the prevailing high wage rates, businessmen found it difficult to make profits by employing their existing labor force. So many jobs were eliminated, and productivity increased, in the effort to ensure solvency.[20]

Since 1980 wage awards have fallen dramatically. This newly found "realism" will have the effect of slowing the rise, stabilizing and eventually (probably in this coming year) reducing the number of jobless. Both industry and labor have learned the hard lesson; the government will not inflate and ratify any more 20 percent increases in wage rates. Now 5 to 7 percent is the still declining norm. Credibility came at last.

A CREDIBLE CONCLUSION

Governments are not born with the silver tongue of credibility. They have to earn it. It is acquired in the hard school of experience. And such credibility is the more difficult to earn when history is replete with failures of both nerve and resolve. I believe that both enemies and friends are now convinced that credibility is established. Mrs. Thatcher's enemies view the phenomenon with a mixture of fury and fascination. Her friends regard it with admiration modified only by nagging anxiety.

For my own part, I am convinced that the great reform will continue. There is much more to be done in the next four or five years than has been accomplished in the last four. The renaissance of Britain, which once seemed an impossible dream, now appears not only feasible but perhaps even likely. Isn't that nice?

NOTES

1. The system of quid pro quo is complex. It ranges from the use of the honors system to the subtleties of information (nods and winks) and attitude appreciation. Alas, here is another underresearched field.

2. French concoctions have long been a source of intoxication to British intelligentsia. Even many steady Conservative heads were now turned by the apparent potency of French planning.

3. Probably the apotheosis of the go-go-growth men was in 1965, as set out in W. Beckerman et al., *The British Economy in 1965* (Cambridge University Press for the National Institute of Economic and Social Research, 1965). In that volume the most distinguished members of the economics profession set out their prescriptions for the newly elected Labour government. More aggregate demand was the basic ingredient together with a "much to be desired" control of income and prices. I remarked in a 1966 review article (*Journal of the Royal Statistical Society*, series A, vol. 129, pt. 2, pp. 275-80) that "exchange rate does not even appear in the index . . . nor does devaluation, money or monetary policy. It is a pity that some of us who read this valuable study should have to suspend belief at Chapter II."

4. I date the first intensive go-go policy as that of Mr. Reginald Maudling in 1963—although a good case can be made for the real start of such policies as dating from the Macmillan government of the post-Suez period, particularly 1958-1959. The Maudling "go-for-growth" policy blighted much of the new (1964) Labour government's policy—particularly since Harold Wilson was unwilling to devalue sterling until forced to do so in 1967. The next disastrous attempt was the Heath-Barber expansion of 1971-1973, which was quickly followed by the very short-lived expansions of Labour governments in 1975 and 1978. Then came the go-go men with the persistent chorus of professional economists; they make their voices heard in Parliament and press and occasionally parade their wares on television.

5. The prize for the most flexible government of the postwar years must go to Mr. Edward Heath's Conservative government of 1970-1974. After promising to reduce the (5-6 percent) rate of inflation "at a stroke," the government started

the greatest inflationary surge of the money supply ever about fifteen months later; similarly, after professing that it would never have wages and price controls, it duly imposed them in mid-1973, and so on.

6. There has long been a controversy over whether the trades unions "cause" inflation (according to Professor Hayek) or whether the appropriate culprit is the monetary authorities through their increase of the rate of growth of the money stock (the Professor Friedman version). On my interpretation, both are causes of inflation but must be interpreted as at different levels. If trades union power were eliminated, for example, this would not necessarily result in an inflation-free economy. The monetary authorities might still conduct expansionist policies and promote inflation; but one important inducement for monetary laxity would be removed. Whatever the power of trades unions, however, inflation can be restrained or eliminated by a suitable monetary policy; but this will be done at a cost, both economic and political, that might well be substantial or, as Hayek has argued, virtually insupportable.

7. In 1981 and 1982 the inevitable reply appeared: "Thatcher Rules, O.K.?" The graffitistes were right again.

8. I am sure you will all realize that it is difficult for me to be objective in judging the success of these policies over the last four years. I will try. But I am equally certain that you will all make adequate allowances for my prejudices.

9. It is noteworthy that many commentators, who had not forecast such a decline in the rate of inflation, nevertheless attributed the decline to the severe depression of 1980–1981 rather than to monetary control. (A recent apologist along these lines is John Williamson in the *Washington Post*, October 15, 1983.) Such commentators did not explain, however, why countries that experienced similar or even more precipitous declines in GDP or increase of unemployment (in 1982), such as Mexico, Brazil, Argentina, and Israel, did not enjoy low inflation or stable prices. Of course, there are special explanations. There always are.

10. It is also worth noting that the 1981 recession was much worse in employment terms than that of 1975, so that the expectation was of a somewhat *higher* ratio of public spending.

11. There were, however, many transitory programs to deal with employment. The only substantial permanent new program, however, was the Youth Training Scheme, designed to train school leavers in working disciplines and skills.

12. Those corporations that were sold have fared extraordinarily well. For example, 49 percent of Cable and Wireless was sold in October 1981 for £182 million, with the government retaining 45 percent of the shares. But today that 45 percent is valued by the market at £560 million. A supply-side miracle indeed!

13. One testament to the success of selling the houses is that there are proposals in the Labour party for embracing a watered-down version of the same policy. The ultimate accolade is emulation.

14. Such timing is, of course, a godsend to journalists and the politicized academic. The temptation has been too much to resist: see, for example, W. Buiter and M. Miller, "The Economic Consequences of Mrs. Thatcher" (mimeo-

graphed), Brookings Panel of Economic Activity, Washington, D.C., September 1983. It is remarkable how even the most sympathetic observers, such as George F. Will (*Washington Post*, September 29, 1983), are misled into comparing the fraction of public spending (or taxation) in the 1979 boom year of the election with the subsequent slump years of 1981 or 1982. And the comparison of the Thatcher record with the peak of 1979 is the standard method of a distinguished journalist Peter Riddell in *The Thatcher Government* (Oxford: Martin Robertson, 1983).

15. This was about par for the decade of the 1970s, when real growth was about 1 to 1.5 percent per annum—most of which was recorded in the Heath-Barber boom of 1971–1973. The critics of Mrs. Thatcher have recourse to two other arguments (that is to say, other than the rather obvious comparison of peak with trough): First, there is a tendency to concentrate the comparison on *manufactured* output, where the decline has been precipitate. Second, there is a common practice of ignoring the oil and gas industries. (For examples of this statistical editing, see Buiter and Miller, "Economic Consequences.") Britain, like many another developed country, has been moving resources out of traditional manufacturing industry into services and oil. To assess a country's performance by reference to its output of manufactures alone makes as much sense as a judgment by reference to textile production or the output of transistor radios. Similarly, to ignore gas and oil, which absorb such substantial resources, makes as much sense as judging Kuwait only by its production of pitted dates and calving camels.

16. For manufacturing industry, productivity increased by 1 percent for the years 1975–1980. But for 1980–1983 the average increase was 5.5 percent, and, as I talk, the rate *still* seems to be rising.

17. Any independent observer will note that, over the period 1979–1983, and particularly in 1981–1983, there has been a marked increase in unemployment in virtually all countries. Britain in 1979–1980 was the earliest to experience substantial increases in unemployment—hence the chorus of "Thatcher is to blame" in 1980–1981. In view of the very rapid rise in unemployment in continental Europe, Canada, and the United States during 1982 (far higher in percentage terms than in the United Kingdom), in order to maintain the original 1980–1981 "Thatcher is to blame" thesis, the critics resorted to the argument that either the *increase* in unemployment or the *level* of unemployment was so much greater in Britain than in comparable countries and therefore attributable to monetarism, Thatcherism, and so on. In view of the varying definitions of unemployment, such arguments become very slippery fish indeed. For a counterexample, the highest rates of recorded unemployment are in Eire and in the Benelux countries, particularly the Netherlands and Belgium. (Probably the greatest increase is in the Netherlands, followed by Belgium and Eire.) But all these countries have had enormous expansionary budgetary policies, exactly the opposite of maligned Thatcherism, over the past four years. And Eire has joined Italy at the top of the European league of inflation rankings and has devalued the punt much as the Thatcher critics wished. Even in the case of Germany, it appears that were one to add in the departed *Gästarbeiter*, the percentage of

Library of
Davidson College

unemployment at the end of 1982 was not far off that of the United Kingdom. It is not clear whether the critics would accept the expansionist policies of Mitterrand's first year as the epitome of the appropriate policy (although most of what is said is consistent with that view). Clearly Mitterrand's policy of expanding the public payroll and incurring massive budget deficits did arrest the increase in unemployment in 1982—but it would be unwise to imagine that the present 10 percent or so will not increase as a consequence of the new tighter policy since mid-1982.

18. The figures for December in each year for Great Britain are, in thousands:

	Unemployed	Increase
1979	1,201	
		810
1980	2,011	
		652
1981	2,663	
		322
1982	2,985	

19. It is true that from mid-1979 onward there was a considerable monetary squeeze—reflected *inter alia* in the narrow monetary aggregates and in the very steep appreciation of sterling but not in the target broad aggregate sterling M_3. As I argued at the American Enterprise Institute late in 1980, monetary policy was tight, not loose, and the dramatic fall in employment could be in some part a consequence of this squeeze. Although I still believe that this judgment was correct and apparently it is now more or less accepted by many commentators, I do not think that the monetary policy, operating through the exchange rate, had in the event nearly as much influence on exports and imports as I then thought. To illustrate, Britain in 1982, when the appreciated sterling would be expected to have decimated trade balances, actually maintained its share of world manufactured exports—and overall there was a record surplus on the current balance (£6 billion or $11 billion) in 1981 and another substantial surplus (£4 billion or $7 billion) in 1982.

20. There is also another side. Some workers found it unprofitable to offer their labor services at the going wage in the nonunionized sector. This was probably a small factor, however, in the increase in unemployment in 1980.